Searchlight BOOKS™

How Does Government Work?

Getting Elected

A Look at Running for Office

Robin Nelson and Sandy Donovan

Lerner Publications Company
Minneapolis

Copyright © 2012 by Sandy Donovan

Lerner Publications Company
A division of Lerner Publishing Group, Inc.
241 First Avenue North
Minneapolis, MN 55401 U.S.A.

Website address: www.lernerbooks.com

Library of Congress Cataloging-in-Publication Data

Nelson, Robin, 1971–
       Getting elected: a look at running for office / by Robin Nelson and Sandy Donovan.
          p.   cm. — (Searchlight books™—How does government work?)
       Includes index.
       ISBN 978-0-7613-6519-8 (lib. bdg. : alk. paper)
       1. Political campaigns—United States—Juvenile literature. 2. Campaign management—United States—Juvenile literature. 3. Elections—United States— Juvenile literature. I. Donovan, Sandra, 1967– II. Title
    JK2281.N45 2012
    324.70973—dc22   2010041859

Manufactured in the United States of America
1 – DP – 12/31/11

Contents

Chapter 1

ELECTIONS IN A DEMOCRACY

The United States is a democracy. In a democracy, the government is run for the people and by the people. But people don't do all the work. They choose representatives to make decisions for them. These people help the government do its job.

Government representatives take the oath of office. This is a promise to do their jobs well. What do representatives do?

Two children look on as their mother casts her vote.

People elect representatives. That means they pick them by voting. In the United States, we elect presidents, members of Congress (the Senate and the House of Representatives), and governors. We also elect school board members and judges.

Who Can Vote?

Voting is a right and a duty of people in a democracy. All U.S. citizens over the age of eighteen can vote.

THESE HIGH SCHOOL SENIORS IN UTAH ARE REGISTERING TO VOTE.

Who Can Run for Office?

A person running for office is called a candidate. To be elected to most offices, candidates must be a certain age. They must be U.S. citizens. Running for office also takes hard work.

We're going to follow Kate Brown (a fictional character) as she runs for the U.S. Senate. As we'll see, Brown finds that running for office is hard but rewarding. Elected officials get to help decide how to make a town, a state, or even the whole country a better place to live.

Carol Moseley Braun of Illinois talks to reporters. She hopes to be elected mayor of Chicago.

CAROL★ FOR CHICAGO
CAROL MOSELEY BRAUN FOR MAYOR

Chapter 2

BROWN FOR SENATE

Brown has been the mayor of Hillville for six years. Her main job has been to listen to the people of Hillville. She helps solve their problems. She also makes sure that city departments, such as the fire department, are running smoothly.

Brown likes being mayor. She feels she's made a difference in people's lives. Most people say she's done a good job.

Mayor Richard M. Daley visits a school in Chicago. Do you know what a mayor's main job is?

Brown feels ready for a bigger challenge. She'd like to help improve the rest of the state and the country. She wants to be one of the two senators her state sends to Washington, D.C. That's where Congress meets. If elected, Brown can help make laws in Congress that will improve more people's lives.

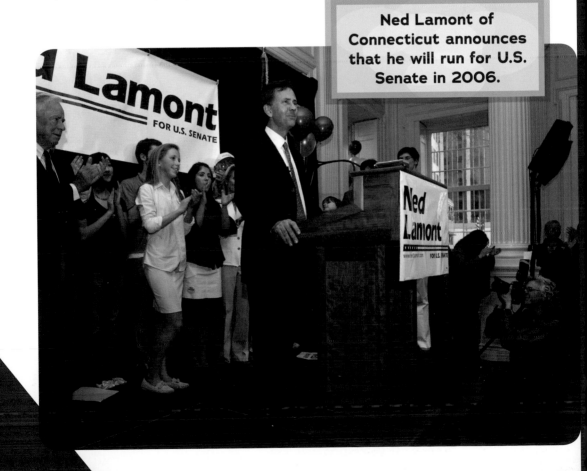

Ned Lamont of Connecticut announces that he will run for U.S. Senate in 2006.

Hard Work

Brown knows running for office is hard. But she's used to working long hours. When she ran for mayor, she often slept just four hours a night. During the day, she campaigned. Campaigning includes all the work of running for office. It includes meeting voters and giving speeches.

But running for the Senate will be tougher than running for mayor. Brown will need to win votes across the state, not just in Hillville. Many people don't know who Brown is.

When Barack Obama ran for president in 2008, he met with voters across the country.

Brown will have to spend money on her campaign. Most voters get information about a candidate from advertising. Brown will have to spend money on TV, radio, and Internet ads.

AN AD FOR U.S. SENATE CANDIDATE SHARRON ANGLE IS ON THE SIDE OF THIS TRUCK.

Parties

The United States has two main political parties. They are the Democratic Party and the Republican Party. Other parties are called third parties. The Green Party is a third party. Political parties are groups of people who join together to gain control over government. Members of a party have similar beliefs about the way government should work. Brown belongs to the Democratic Party.

This artwork shows the symbols for the Republican Party (TOP) and the Democratic Party (BOTTOM).

U.S. Senate candidate Hillary Clinton shares her ideas with the voters of New York in 2000.

Democratic Party leaders told Brown this is the right time for her to run for the Senate. They like her ideas about how to improve the government.

It's Official

Brown has decided to run next year. Her family and friends said they would support her. They'll work hard to help her win.

Family support is important to candidates. Baltimore, Maryland, governor Martin O'Malley stands with his wife, daughters, and sons after announcing his reelection campaign.

Florida governor Charlie Crist announced his plans to run for the U.S. Senate in 2010.

It's time to get to work. Brown calls a press conference to announce her candidacy. At press conferences, people answer questions from reporters. Reporters from around the state come to hear Brown's announcement and to report what she has to say.

Vice presidential candidate Dick Cheney thanks volunteers and staff who worked on his 2000 election campaign.

Finding Good Help

Brown's press conference is in March. The election will be in November of next year. Brown has almost two years of campaigning ahead of her.

Brown is ready to work. But she knows she can't win this election by herself. She'll need a staff to run her campaign.

The first person Brown looks for is a campaign manager. He or she will manage the details of the campaign. The next person Brown finds is a fund-raiser. This person will be in charge of raising money to pay for the campaign. Finally, Brown picks her treasurer. The treasurer keeps track of campaign money and pays the bills.

AL GORE RAN FOR PRESIDENT IN 2000. HERE HE INTRODUCES HIS CAMPAIGN MANAGER, DONNA BRAZILE.

Chapter 3

CAMPAIGNING

The work of campaigning is just beginning. On Election Day, Brown will face two opponents for the Senate seat. One is Senator Charles Howe. He is running for reelection. He's a Republican. The other is a Green Party member named Ryan Hu.

South Carolina candidate for governor Nikki Haley watches election results with her family and supporters. What are some things candidates do to try to get elected?

During a 1992 debate, presidential candidates (FROM LEFT TO RIGHT) **Ross Perot, Bill Clinton, and George H. W. Bush** discuss issues of importance to voters.

The Issues

For the next several months, the candidates will discuss issues that affect voters. Each candidate will try to convince voters that his or her beliefs about the issues are what's best for the state and the country. Brown tells voters her beliefs on health care, jobs, and the environment.

On the Campaign Trail

Brown knows she can't waste time. Her campaign has to tell voters why she should be the next senator. To do this, her staff members plan campaign activities. They run TV and radio ads. The ads talk about Brown's success as mayor. They explain how Brown will be a better senator than Howe has been.

Staff members of Colin Wong hand out information about Wong's ideas. He ran for state senator of Hawaii in 2004.

Candidates meet with voters out in public. U.S. Senator Barbara Boxer of California holds a baby in 2010.

Brown's days are full. Every morning, she gets up early and meets with her staff. As mayor of Hillville, Brown has city business to take care of during the day. She wants to make sure she's still doing a good job as mayor.

In the evenings, Brown campaigns. She travels to meet voters. She gives several speeches a week.

Raising Money

Brown's fund-raiser works on raising money for her campaign. Fund-raising events are one way to get money. Brown's campaign raises lots of money by holding fancy dinners for wealthy Democrats.

Sometimes politicians attend fund-raisers for candidates in their own parties. In 1995 Vice President Al Gore (RIGHT) went to a fund-raiser for Jerry Estruth, who was running for U.S. Senator of California.

Brown's campaign also gets smaller donations from others. Staff members call people and send letters asking for donations.

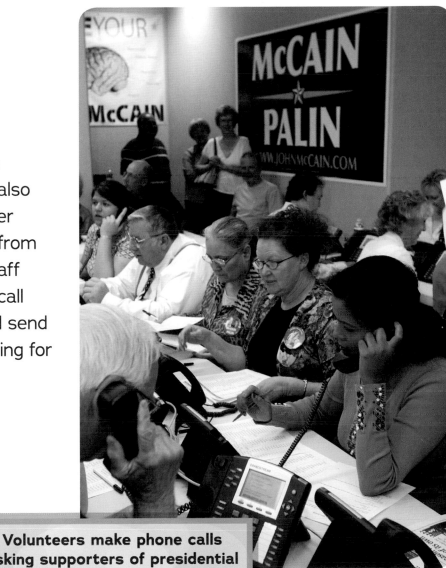

Volunteers make phone calls asking supporters of presidential candidate John McCain to donate money for the campaign.

Chapter 4

THE FINISH LINE

In the days before the election, Brown is busier than ever. She attends meetings called rallies.

Senator Paul Wellstone (LEFT) of Minnesota greets supporters at a rally in 1996. Why do voters go to rallies?

At a rally in California, supporters cheer candidate for governor Meg Whitman.

Rallies take place in malls, town halls, and other spots. Voters go to rallies to show support for a candidate. Brown gives a speech, and the crowd cheers.

Election Day

After a blur of speeches and rallies, Election Day arrives. Election Day is Brown's last chance to convince people to vote for her.

In some places, campaigning on Election Day is illegal. But it's not illegal in Hillville. So Brown wakes early and meets with her campaign manager. They discuss their campaign plans for the day.

Campaign volunteer Charlie Warner (RIGHT) of Nevada calls voters on Election Day.

At seven in the morning, Brown goes to her polling place. This is where people vote. News cameras film her walking in. When she comes out, she smiles at the cameras.

Barack Obama's daughters Malia (LEFT) and Sasha (RIGHT) watch as their father casts his vote in the 2008 presidential election.

New York mayor Michael Bloomberg shakes hands with voters on Election Day.

Next, Brown goes to a rally outside Hillville City Hall. Hundreds of supporters there cheer for her. After the rally, Brown talks to as many people as possible. She walks down the streets and asks people to support her. Many people want to shake her hand. They wish her luck in the election.

Meanwhile, Brown's staff is hard at work. Staff members will try to get as many of Brown's supporters to the polling places as they can.

CAMPAIGN WORKERS GIVE THEIR CANDIDATES ONE LAST SHOW OF SUPPORT AS VOTERS HEAD INTO POLLING PLACES.

Election Night

Brown spends the day going to rallies and giving speeches. At eight in the evening, the polling places close. Brown waits for the results. Voting areas across the state report their results slowly. By eight thirty, just a few areas have reported their votes. Senator Howe is winning. Brown is in second place. The Green Party candidate is in third. But it's too early for Brown to be worried. Results have just begun to come in.

Voters can watch the election results on TV. The red places on this map from the 1984 presidential election show states in which Ronald Reagan won the most votes.

Candidate Michael Bennett and his wife and daughters watch election results to see if Bennett will be the next senator from Colorado.

By ten, half the voting areas have reported their votes. Howe and Brown are tied. Soon Brown begins to take a lead. By the time most of the votes are counted, reporters are saying Brown will win.

Brown hugs her family. But it isn't time to announce her victory yet. Friends and staff members call to congratulate her. She tells them it isn't over, but she knows she has won.

PEOPLE WATCH ELECTION RESULTS IN TIMES SQUARE IN NEW YORK CITY TO SEE WHO WILL WIN THE 2008 PRESIDENTIAL ELECTION.

Sharron Angle of Nevada speaks to supporters after learning that her opponent in the race for U.S. Senator has won.

At ten thirty, an important phone call comes. It's Senator Howe. He's calling to concede. This means he'll publicly announce that he has lost the election. He too knows Brown has won. Howe congratulates Brown. He tells her she ran a good campaign.

Victory Party

By quarter of eleven, supporters have gathered to celebrate Brown's victory. Brown and her family enter the victory party. They wave to the crowd. The crowd cheers wildly.

Ronald Reagan celebrates his victory in the 1980 presidential election.

Brown gives her victory speech. She thanks her family and her staff for their work. She says she couldn't have won without them.

Barack Obama speaks to his supporters in Chicago's Grant Park after he was elected president in 2008.

U.S. Senator Elizabeth Dole takes the oath of office in 1993. Her husband, Bob Dole (CENTER), looks on.

What Happens Next?

After almost two years of campaigning, Kate Brown has won the election. In January, she'll go to Washington, D.C. She will begin her term as Senator Brown. She will have offices in Washington and in Hillville.

Before long, Brown will think about running for reelection. She knows firsthand that campaigning is hard. She'll have to decide if she'll do it all again.

Norm Coleman of Minnesota ran for reelection as senator in 2008.

Glossary

campaign: a series of actions organized over a period of time to win an election

candidate: a person who runs for office

citizen: a person who lives in a city, a state, or a country

concede: to publicly admit defeat in an election

Congress: a group of elected officials who write, talk about, and make laws. The U.S. Congress is made up of the Senate and the House of Representatives.

democracy: a political system in which government is run for the people and by the people

donation: money given to a person or a cause

elect: to pick by voting

fund-raiser: a person whose job is to raise money for a candidate. A fund-raiser is also an event set up by a fund-raiser.

political party: a group of people who join together to gain political power. Members of political parties have similar beliefs about the way the government should be run.

polling place: the official place where people vote in their neighborhood

press conference: a meeting where people answer questions from TV and newspaper reporters

representative: a person who is elected to help the government do its job

staff: a group of people who do paid work for an organization

Learn More about Government

Books

Goodman, Susan E. *See How They Run: Campaign Dreams, Election Schemes, and the Race to the White House*. New York: Bloomsbury, 2008. This fun title includes lots of information about elections.

Nelson, Robin, and Sandy Donovan. *The Congress: A Look at the Legislative Branch*. Minneapolis: Lerner Publications Company, 2012. Read all about the Congress, the part of government that character Kate Brown joined when she got elected.

Stier, Catherine. *If I Ran for President*. Morton Grove, IL: Albert Whitman, 2007. In this lively book, six children explain the election process.

Sutcliffe, Jane. *Barack Obama*. Minneapolis: Lerner Publications Company, 2010. Read the life story of Barack Obama, from his childhood in Hawaii and Indonesia to his election as president of the United States.

Websites

Ben's Guide to U.S. Government for Kids
http://bensguide.gpo.gov/3-5/election/index.html
This guide to the U.S. government includes details about the election process.

Kids in the House
http://kids.clerk.house.gov
This website from the U.S. House of Representatives provides educational and entertaining information about the legislative branch of the U.S. government to students of all age levels.

Kids Voting USA
https://netforum.avectra.com/eWeb/StartPage.aspx?Site-KVUSA
This website features information on how kids can get involved in elections around the country.

Index

Photo Acknowledgments

The images in this book are used with the permission of: AP Photo/Charles Dharapak, p. 4;
© Jewel Samad/AFP/Getty Images, p. 5; AP Photo/The Salt Lake Tribune, Scott Sommerdorf, p. 6;
© Scott Olson/Getty Images, p. 7; © Barry Brecheisen/Getty Images, p. 8; © Darren McCollester/
Getty Images, p. 9; © Chip Somodevilla/Getty Images, p. 10; © Ethan Miller/Getty Images, pp. 11,
23; © Matthew Trommer/Dreamstime.com, p. 12; © Timothy A. Clary/AFP/Getty Images, p. 13; AP
Photo/Gail Burton, p. 14; © Joe Raedle/Getty Images, pp. 15, 27; © Paul Buck/AFP/Getty Images,
p. 16; © Luke Frazza/AFP/Getty Images, p. 17; AP Photo/David Goldman, p. 18; © Eugene Garcia/
AFP/Getty Images, p. 19; AP Photo/Lucy Pemoni, p. 20; © Kevork Djansezian/Getty Images, p. 21;
AP Photo/Susan Ragan, p. 22; AP Photo/Andy King, p. 24; AP Photo/Lenny Ignelzi, p. 25; © Melina
Mara/The Washington Post via Getty Images, p. 26; © Craig Warga/NY Daily News Archive via
Getty Images, p. 28; © Christopher Capozziello/Getty Images, p. 29; © Robert Maass/CORBIS,
p. 30; © Matt McClain/Getty Images, p. 31; © Jemal Countess/Getty Images, p. 32; © Robyn Beck/
AFP/Getty Images, p. 33; AP Photo, p. 34; © Anthony Jacobs/Getty Images, p. 35; © Mark Wilson/
Getty Images, p. 36; AP Photo/Winona Daily News, Melissa Carlo, p. 37.

Front cover: AP Photo/David Goldman (top); © Ken Skalski/CORBIS (bottom).

Main body text set in Adrianna Regular 14/20
Typeface provided by Chank